LIGHT THE MENORAH!

For Willa and Nathan –JJ

Candle-lighting blessings, songs and recipes from *All About Hanukkah*, by
Judyth Groner and Madeline Wikler ©1999 Kar-Ben Publishing
Crafts from *Jewish Holiday Crafts for Little Hands* by Ruth Esrig Brinn
© 1993 Kar-Ben Publishing

KAR-BEN PUBLISHING, INC.
A division of Lerner Publishing Group, Inc.
241 First Avenue North
Minneapolis, MN 55401 USA
1-800-4-KARBEN

Website address: www.karben.com

Main bodytext set in Garamond 3 LT Std 16/19.
Typeface provided by Adobe Systems.

Library of Congress Cataloging-in-Publication Data

Names: Jules, Jacqueline, 1956- author. | Swarner, Kristina, illustrator.
Title: Light the menorah! / by Jacqueline Jules ; illustrated by Kristina Swarner.
Description: Minneapolis : Kar-Ben Publishing, [2018] | Audience: Ages 4-10 ;
    grades 4 to 6.
Identifiers: LCCN 2017030345| ISBN 9781512483680 (pbk.: alk. paper) |
    ISBN 9781512483697 (pb) | ISBN 9781541524040 (eb pdf)
Subjects: LCSH: Hanukkah—Juvenile literature.
Classification: LCC BM695.H3 J85 2018 | DDC 296.4/35—dc23

LC record available at https://lccn.loc.gov/2017030345

Manufactured in the United States of America
1-43364-33176-12/6/2017

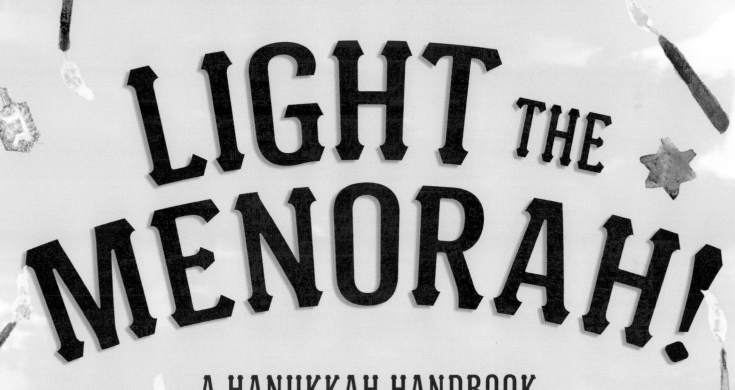

LIGHT THE MENORAH!

A HANUKKAH HANDBOOK

Jacqueline Jules
illustrations by Kristina Swarner

KAR-BEN
PUBLISHING

INTRODUCTION

The moments before lighting the Hanukkah candles are a time of reflection. Before we say the blessings, we consider the story of the Maccabees and their courage to fight for religious freedom. We remember their faith in lighting the Temple menorah even when they did not have enough oil. We imagine their wonder as they watched a flame burn miraculously longer than expected.

The Hanukkah rituals are worth thinking about. Why do we line up the candles in the Hanukkah menorah from right to left, but light them from left to right? Why are we careful not to blow out the candles until they have finished burning? What is the role of the shamash, the helper candle? Can our Hanukkah traditions inspire us to be more thoughtful throughout the year?

In the following pages, you will find a brief reflection to read aloud just before you recite the blessings and light the Hanukkah candles. This book also offers Hanukkah basics, instructions for playing dreidel, songs, recipes, and crafts to enhance your celebration. May *Light the Menorah!* give you the tools for meaningful family moments in the light of your menorah.

CANDLE BLESSINGS

As we gather to say the blessings over the Hanukkah candles, the mood should be both solemn and joyful. To create this atmosphere, pause before saying the candle blessings. After the blessings, read the poem and reflection on the following pages for the corresponding night.

We say two blessings each night when we light the Hanukkah candles:

בָּרוּךְ אַתָּה יְיָ אֱלֹהֵינוּ מֶלֶךְ הָעוֹלָם,
אֲשֶׁר קִדְּשָׁנוּ בְּמִצְוֹתָיו וְצִוָּנוּ לְהַדְלִיק נֵר שֶׁל חֲנֻכָּה.

Baruch Atah Adonai Eloheinu Melech Ha'olam, asher kid'shanu b'mitzvotav v'tzivanu l'hadlik ner shel Hanukkah.

We praise You, Adonai our God, Ruler of the Universe, Who makes us holy by Your mitzvot and commands us to light the Hanukkah candles.

בָּרוּךְ אַתָּה יְיָ אֱלֹהֵינוּ מֶלֶךְ הָעוֹלָם,
שֶׁעָשָׂה נִסִּים לַאֲבוֹתֵינוּ בַּיָּמִים הָהֵם בַּזְּמַן הַזֶּה.

Baruch Atah Adonai Eloheinu Melech Ha'olam, she'asah nisim la'avoteinu bayamim hahem baz'man hazeh.

We praise You, Adonai our God, Ruler of the Universe, for the miracles which You performed for our ancestors in those days.

On the first night we add this blessing:

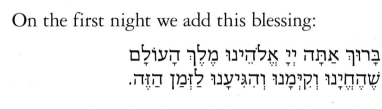

בָּרוּךְ אַתָּה יְיָ אֱלֹהֵינוּ מֶלֶךְ הָעוֹלָם
שֶׁהֶחֱיָנוּ וְקִיְּמָנוּ וְהִגִּיעָנוּ לַזְּמַן הַזֶּה.

Baruch Atah Adonai Eloheinu Melech Ha'olam,
shehecheyanu, v'kiyemanu, v'higi'anu laz'man hazeh.

We praise You, Adonai our God, Ruler of the
Universe, Who kept us alive and well to celebrate
this special time.

Once the candles are lit, it is traditional—and fun!—to play
games and sing Hanukkah songs. See the last pages of this
book for suggestions.

FIRST NIGHT

On this night,
we bless
the first flame.
The light
willing to stand alone—
to speak out
when others stand back—
to burn brightly
when others are indifferent.

REFLECTION FOR THE FIRST NIGHT OF HANUKKAH

At Hanukkah, we recall the Maccabees, the small army of determined fighters who won a battle for religious freedom against King Antiochus in the second century. The holiday celebrates the courage to try even when the odds are against you. Like Judah Maccabee who led his men against a much larger army, someone has to be strong enough to say, "This is wrong and I will do something to help." It is not easy to be first. You don't know if others will join you. And you don't know if you will succeed. But there are times in life when we need to be the first candle, to brighten the darkness the best we can, even if we must stand alone.

SECOND NIGHT

One jar of oil.
too small to last long.

Still, the Maccabees
lit the menorah.

Chose to display
faith not fear.

And the fire
they kindled
continued.

REFLECTION FOR THE SECOND NIGHT OF HANUKKAH

After their victory, the Maccabees went to Jerusalem and found the Temple in ruins. They cleaned it and removed all evidence of idol worship. Then they prepared to rededicate the Temple by lighting a seven-branched candelabrum known as a menorah. According to rabbinic legend, they could only find a small jar of purified oil—enough to last a single day. More oil would take eight days to obtain. Should they put off their celebration or go ahead? The rabbis say the Maccabees chose to light the menorah rather than to allow the Temple to stay in darkness for another week. They had the faith to forge ahead, to decide that it was better to have some light than none at all. To succeed, we must often do the best with what we have.

THIRD NIGHT

The Maccabees
watched with wonder
hour by hour,
day by day—
a flame
defying the darkness,
refusing to die
and quench the faith
they had battled
to preserve.

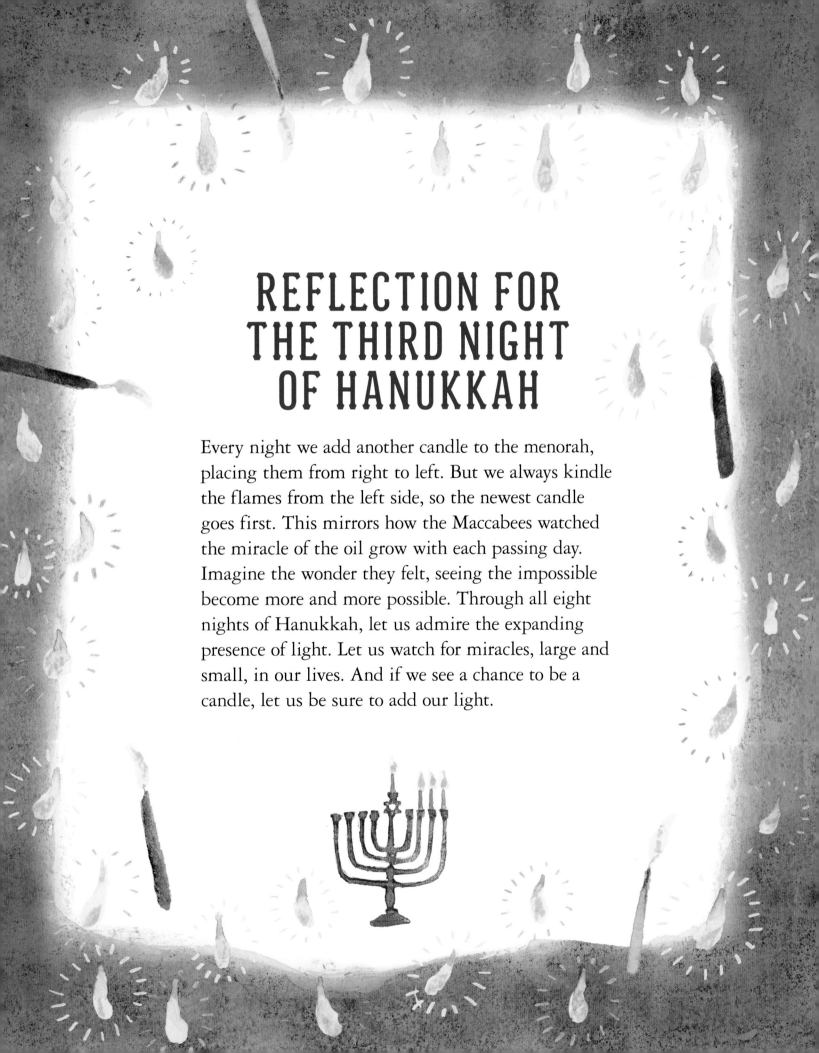

REFLECTION FOR THE THIRD NIGHT OF HANUKKAH

Every night we add another candle to the menorah, placing them from right to left. But we always kindle the flames from the left side, so the newest candle goes first. This mirrors how the Maccabees watched the miracle of the oil grow with each passing day. Imagine the wonder they felt, seeing the impossible become more and more possible. Through all eight nights of Hanukkah, let us admire the expanding presence of light. Let us watch for miracles, large and small, in our lives. And if we see a chance to be a candle, let us be sure to add our light.

FOURTH NIGHT

Wicks lit
from left to right,
not by a match
but by a helper
who lends its flame
just long enough
to make sure others
also have the chance
to glow.

REFLECTION FOR THE FOURTH NIGHT OF HANUKKAH

We light the Hanukkah menorah with a shamash, or helper candle. The shamash is used to make sure the Hanukkah candles do no work. The shamash has a place on the menorah that is apart from the other candles. It is often in the middle and stands a little higher than the other candles. As we light the shamash to begin the candle lighting ceremony, let us remember all the people in our lives who serve and help us—parents, teachers, medical professionals, librarians, police officers, fire fighters, custodial workers, and others. Let us not forget to say "thank you" whenever we can.

FIFTH NIGHT

This moment
is a feather-shaped flame
shining in the sacred space
between yesterday
and tomorrow.

Look into its yellow eye
and see only the light
burning before you.

Let everything else
disappear in the dark.

REFLECTION FOR THE FIFTH NIGHT OF HANUKKAH

It is customary not to work while the candles in the menorah are burning. The average Hanukkah candle lasts less than an hour. Dishes or homework can wait that short time. Play dreidel or a family board game. Sit by the candles and share the events of the day. Spend these light-filled minutes focused on your loved ones. Too many of us spend our days rushing from one activity to another. May the Hanukkah lights remind us to stop and fully appreciate each flickering moment.

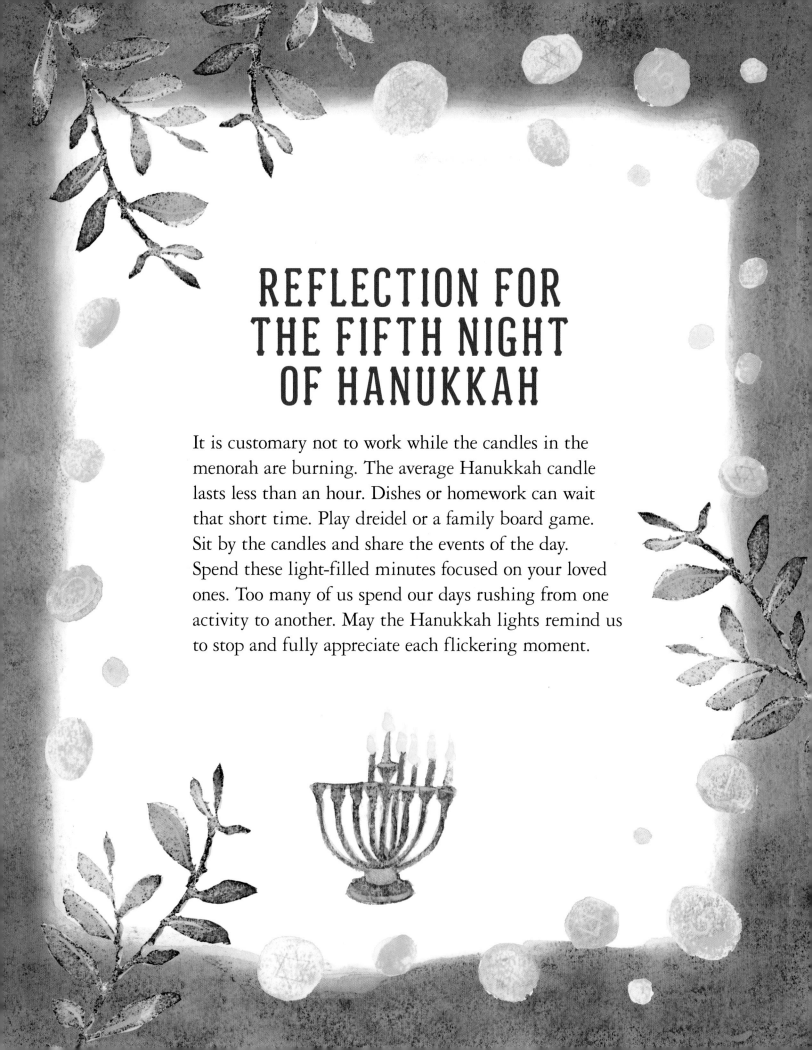

SIXTH NIGHT

A candle wick
requires wax
as fuel for its flame,
just as
the human heart
requires hope,
red hot
at its center,
to keep beating
through dark times.

REFLECTION FOR THE SIXTH NIGHT OF HANUKKAH

Hanukkah candles should be allowed to burn until all the wax is melted. Watch the wick in the center of the flame. It can't produce light without wax serving as fuel. Hanukkah reminds us of the fuel we need to keep going through difficult or disappointing times in our lives. We need hope. We need kindness. Don't be the one to blow out someone else's dreams. Don't be the one who destroys another's faith in goodness. Just as we are instructed to let the Hanukkah candles burn without interference, let us protect the feelings of others. Sometimes that means allowing another person to enjoy more attention. Sometimes it means keeping negative thoughts to ourselves. Be careful not to say things that will extinguish someone else's smile.

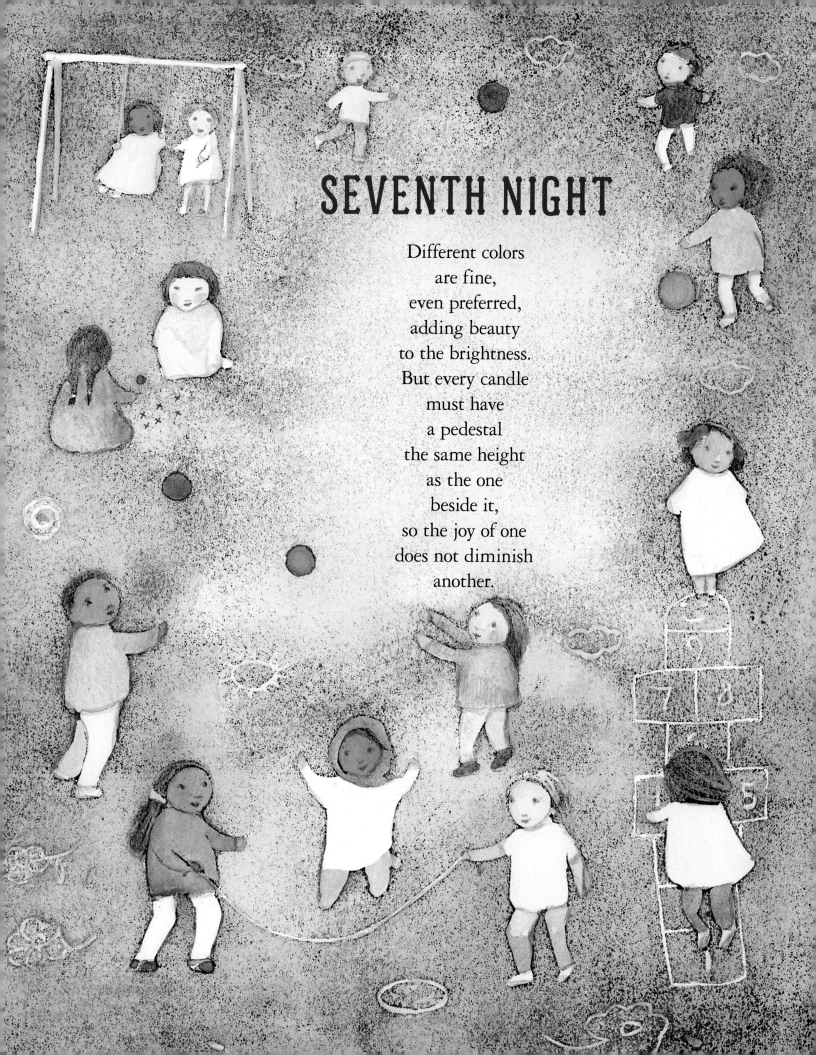

SEVENTH NIGHT

Different colors
are fine,
even preferred,
adding beauty
to the brightness.
But every candle
must have
a pedestal
the same height
as the one
beside it,
so the joy of one
does not diminish
another.

REFLECTION FOR THE SEVENTH NIGHT OF HANUKKAH

A traditional Hanukkah menorah is constructed in such a way that eight candles can be placed in a straight row at an equal height. This means all the lights commemorating the Hanukkah miracle are level with each other and each light has the chance to shine without interference from another. Let this remind us that every life is special. Another person's faith or perspective may not be our own. We may not have the same skin color. But no one person has more right to happiness than another. Our joy should never come at the expense of someone else.

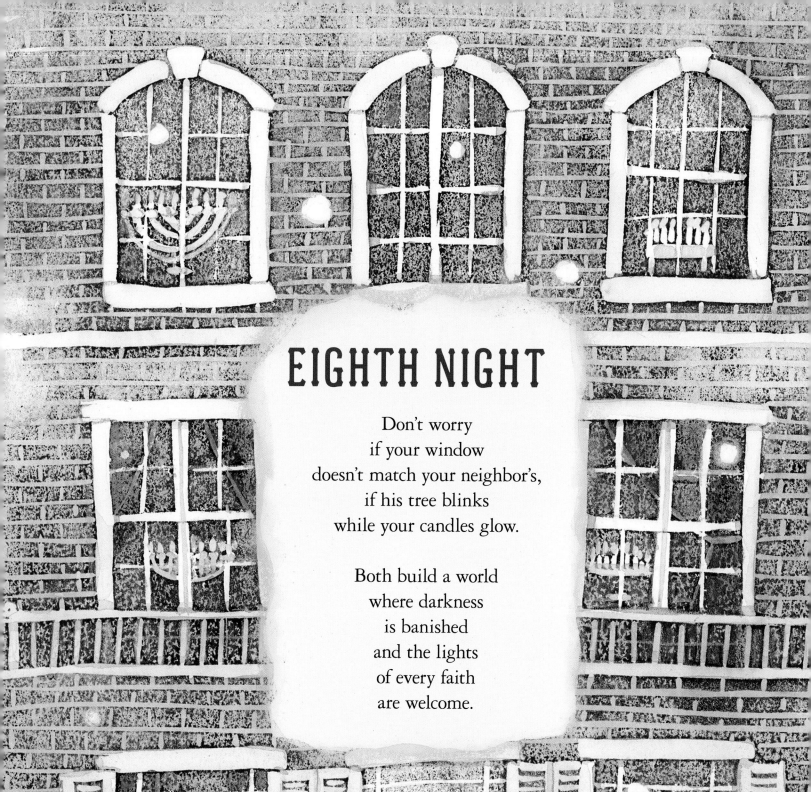

EIGHTH NIGHT

Don't worry
if your window
doesn't match your neighbor's,
if his tree blinks
while your candles glow.

Both build a world
where darkness
is banished
and the lights
of every faith
are welcome.

REFLECTION FOR THE EIGHTH NIGHT OF HANUKKAH

A Hanukkah menorah should be displayed in a window or by the door. Others should be able to see the candles as they pass by your house. With a visible menorah, we are publicizing the story of Hanukkah. We are celebrating faith and courage. And we are demonstrating our belief in every person's right to religious freedom. Be proud of your heritage. Shine your lights in a place where all can see.

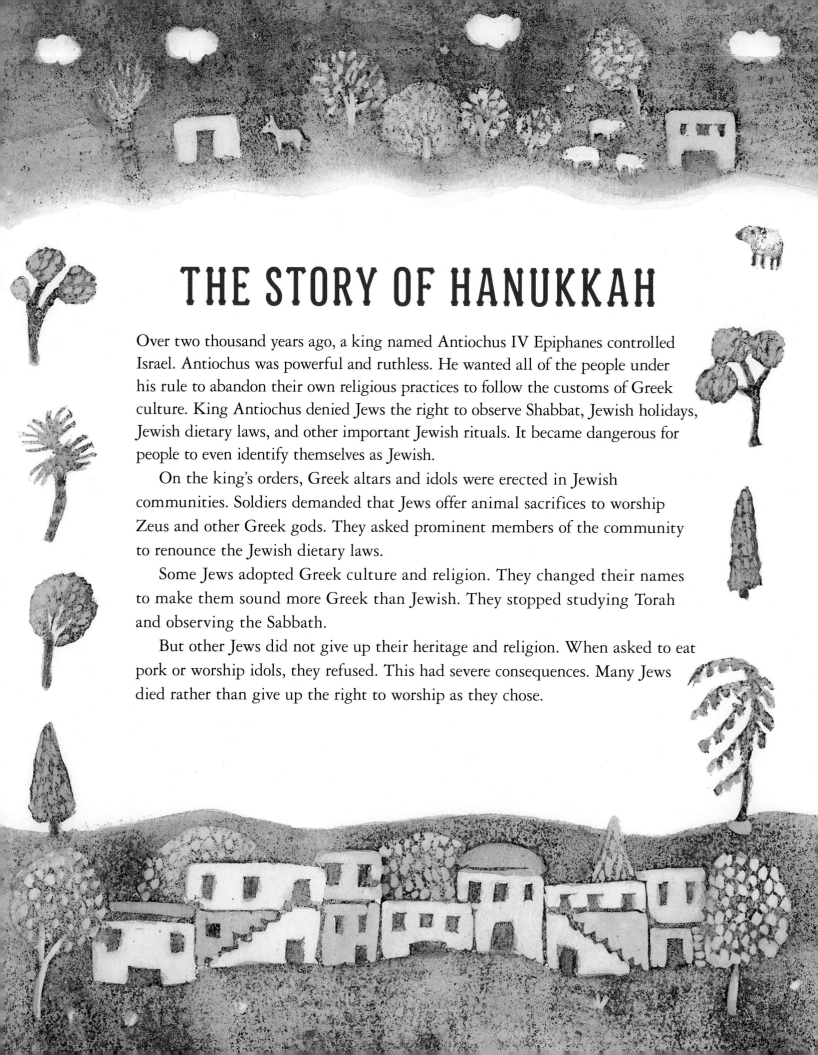

THE STORY OF HANUKKAH

Over two thousand years ago, a king named Antiochus IV Epiphanes controlled Israel. Antiochus was powerful and ruthless. He wanted all of the people under his rule to abandon their own religious practices to follow the customs of Greek culture. King Antiochus denied Jews the right to observe Shabbat, Jewish holidays, Jewish dietary laws, and other important Jewish rituals. It became dangerous for people to even identify themselves as Jewish.

On the king's orders, Greek altars and idols were erected in Jewish communities. Soldiers demanded that Jews offer animal sacrifices to worship Zeus and other Greek gods. They asked prominent members of the community to renounce the Jewish dietary laws.

Some Jews adopted Greek culture and religion. They changed their names to make them sound more Greek than Jewish. They stopped studying Torah and observing the Sabbath.

But other Jews did not give up their heritage and religion. When asked to eat pork or worship idols, they refused. This had severe consequences. Many Jews died rather than give up the right to worship as they chose.

Strong resistance rose up in the countryside, particularly in Modi'in, a town west of Jerusalem where a priest named Mattathias lived with his five sons. Mattathias was well-respected. The king's soldiers wanted him to be the first to step forward and show loyalty to King Antiochus. Mattathias answered loudly and clearly. He would not worship idols or forsake his faith.

With his sons by his side, Mattathias fled to the mountains to organize a revolt against King Antiochus. Already an old man, Mattathias did not live to see the success of his rebellion. When he died, he turned over his leadership to his son, Judah. Judah's bold fighting style earned him the nickname "Maccabee," meaning "hammer."

Judah, his brothers, and growing band of followers waged war against Antiochus. They were called the Maccabees and they found success through night raids and sneak attacks. Their courage fighting a large and well-equipped army inspired Jews all over the country. In one famous battle, the Maccabees even faced soldiers riding trained war elephants.

In 164, B.C.E., after three years of fighting, the Maccabees gained control of the Temple in Jerusalem. This was as much a spiritual victory as a military one. Now the Jews could rededicate their most sacred house of worship. The Temple and its grounds were in terrible condition. The sanctuary was filthy. Ornate doors had been burned. The golden menorah that once burned with seven branches of continuous torch light was gone. The Maccabees tore their clothing as a sign of mourning. They wailed and wept.

Then they got to work. First, they scrubbed the Temple from top to bottom. They pulled weeds and made repairs. They also replaced the ceremonial items that had been stolen from the sanctuary. Some sources say the Maccabees made a makeshift menorah from iron spears. Others say a gold seven-branched lamp was created during the time they built a new altar.

On the 25th of the Hebrew month of Kislev, the new menorah was lit and the Temple was rededicated. In Hebrew, the word, "Hanukkah," means "dedication."

The very first Hanukkah lasted eight days, just like the fall harvest holiday of Sukkot. During wartime, the Maccabees couldn't take a week to observe Sukkot properly, so they celebrated for eight days during the rededication of the Temple. This is the historical view of the first Hanukkah holiday.

However, rabbinic tradition gives another reason for the eight-day celebration. A popular legend says the Maccabees needed oil to light the menorah. They searched the Temple. All they found was one small cruse of sealed, purified oil—only enough to last one day. Instead of delaying their ceremony for eight days until more oil could be obtained, the Maccabees lit the menorah anyway. Miraculously, the small amount of oil burned for eight full days. This legend, known as the "miracle of the oil" encourages us to remember a triumph of faith along with a military conquest.

When we light Hanukkah candles, we are celebrating religious freedom. We are sharing a belief that determined individuals can successfully fight for justice. Hanukkah is also called "The Festival of Lights." May the light of freedom always burn brightly in our homes and in our hearts.

MORE ABOUT HANUKKAH

When does Hanukkah occur?

Jewish holidays follow a calendar with Hebrew names for the months. The year on a Jewish calendar is not the same length as the year on the civil calendar. While Hanukkah always begins on the eve of the 25th day of the Hebrew month of Kislev, the day shifts on the civil calendar. It falls in November or December and can occur as early as Thanksgiving and as late as December 24th. Consult a Jewish calendar or the internet to learn the exact date Hanukkah falls on the civil calendar each year.

Where is Hanukkah celebrated?

Hanukkah is primarily a home celebration. While synagogues may hold latke dinners, public candle-lightings, or other Hanukkah events, there are no religious services specifically for Hanukkah. Jews are permitted to go to work and school during the festival.

Jewish tradition instructs families to say the blessings and light a menorah at home on each night of Hanukkah. During the week, candles are lit after sunset. On Friday night, however, they should be lit before the Shabbat candles. On Saturday night, they should be lit after sundown and the Havdalah ceremony, ending Shabbat.

Many families also choose to exchange gifts on Hanukkah. It is traditional to eat fried foods like potato latkes and donuts because they recall the miracle of the oil. Foil-wrapped chocolates in the shape of coins, known as Hanukkah gelt, are popular treats. Families also like to play the game of dreidel and sing Hanukkah songs.

How many candles are needed to celebrate all eight nights?

On every night of Hanukkah, a helper candle or shamash is lit in addition to the number of nights being celebrated. So on the first night, two candles are needed and on the second night, three candles, etc. A single menorah will require forty-four candles during the eight-day holiday.

Candles are placed in the menorah from right to left. Light the shamash first. Then kindle the other lights from left to right.

Why do Jews play dreidel at Hanukkah time?

The Hebrew letters on the dreidel, *Nun, Gimel, Hey, Shin* represent the Hebrew sentence *"Nes gadol hayah sham"* which means "a great miracle happened there." Depending on your perspective, this can refer to the victory of the Maccabees or the miracle of the oil. In Israel, dreidels have different letters—*Nun, Gimel, Hey, Pey*—which translates to "a great miracle happened *here.*"

Some rabbis taught that Jews used the dreidel game to provide a cover for religious study. If soldiers investigated a group of scholars, they would take out their dreidels and pretend to be gambling instead of engaging in the illegal activity of studying Torah.

Other histories say the custom of playing dreidel at Hanukkah was borrowed from a European gambling game with a spinning top called teetotum. Using the same rules as dreidel, teetotum was often enjoyed during the winter solstice season. A German version of the game used the letters, N, G, H, and S, supporting the suggestion that European Jews adapted dreidel from their neighbors long after Maccabean times.

What role did women play in the Hanukkah story?

Two stories of courageous women are often told at Hanukkah time.

One is a legend. It tells the story of Judith, a wealthy widow who took it upon herself to save her town of Bethulia when it was surrounded by Assyrian forces led by General Holofernes. With food and water supplies cut off, the Jewish mayor, Uzziah, planned to surrender in five days. But Judith devised a clever plan. She slipped into the enemy camp and approached Holofernes, pretending to be a spy. Since she was a beautiful woman, Holofernes was intrigued. He allowed her into his tent and accepted her food and wine. When he fell asleep, Judith killed him, saving her people from destruction.

Another Hanukkah story recalls the steadfast courage of Hannah, the mother of seven sons who refused to bow down to Greek idols. Hannah's defiance ended in tragedy, but her fierce commitment to Jewish law is honored and remembered.

Where is the Hanukkah story recorded?

The story of Hanukkah is not found in the Torah, the Five Books of Moses. Instead, information about Hanukkah is found in post-biblical texts. A body of literature called the Apocrypha contains two books describing the revolt of Mattathias and his sons against King Antiochus. They do not contain any mention of the miracle of the oil. That story comes from the Talmud, a collection of important work by rabbinic scholars written centuries after the Maccabean victory.

The stories of Judith and Hannah are also found in the Apocrypha.

THE DREIDEL GAME

A dreidel is a spinning top with a Hebrew letter on each of its four sides: *Nun, Gimel, Hey, Shin*. These letters represent the Hebrew phrase, "*Nes Gadol Hayah Sham*," which means "A Great Miracle Happened There." (In Israel, the dreidel's fourth letter is a *Pey* rather than a *Shin*, to represent the Hebrew phrase, "A Great Miracle Happened *Here*.")

The game of dreidel can be played with 2-6 players. Every player starts with an equal number of pennies, raisins, peanuts, marbles, or any other small items to serve as playing tokens.

To start the game, each player puts a token into the middle to create a "pot."

The first player spins the dreidel and waits for it to fall on one side.

If the dreidel lands on *Nun*, the player does *Nothing*.

If the dreidel lands on *Gimel*, the player *Gets* everything in the pot and the players must all contribute a token to begin a new pot.

If the dreidel lands on *Hey*, the player takes *Half* of the pot.

If the dreidel lands on *Shin*, the player *Sacrifices* a token, putting it into the pot.

The player who has the most tokens wins the game.

ש   ה   ג   נ

Shin   **Hey**   **Gimel**   **Nun**

HANUKKAH SONGS

Ma'Oz Tzur

Traditional

Hanukkah, Oh Hanukkah

Folk Song   Yiddish lyrics by Mordkhe Rivesman

Oh Ha-nu-kkah, Oh Ha-nu-kkah, come light the me-no-rah__, Lets__ have a par-ty, we'll all dance the ho-rah. Ga-ther round the ta-ble, we'll give you a treat: Drei-dels to play with and lat-kes to eat. And while we are play-ing, The can-dles are burn-ing__ low. One for each night, they will shed a sweet light to re-

1. mind us of days long a-go__.
2. mind us of days long a-go.

Khanike, Oy Khanike,
A yontif a sheyner.
A lustiger, a freilicher nito noch a zoeyner.
Alle nacht in dreidlach shpiln mir.
Zudig heyse latkes ess un a shir.

Geshvinder tzindt kinder
Di dinike lichtecha ohn.
Zogt "Al hanisim," loibt Gott far di nisim
Un kumt gicher tantzen in kohn.

HANUKKAH RECIPES

Potato Latkes

Ingredients:

  3 large potatoes (2 c. grated)

  Small onion

  2 eggs

  2 Tbsp. flour or matzah meal

  1 tsp. salt

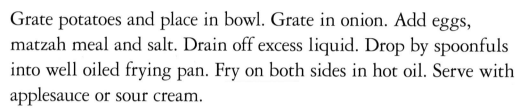

Grate potatoes and place in bowl. Grate in onion. Add eggs, matzah meal and salt. Drain off excess liquid. Drop by spoonfuls into well oiled frying pan. Fry on both sides in hot oil. Serve with applesauce or sour cream.

No-Peel Latkes

Ingredients:

  1 egg

  1 small onion quartered

  3 c. unpeeled potatoes, cubed

  2 Tbsp. flour

  1 Tbsp. oil

  ¼ Tbsp. sugar

  ½ tsp. salt

  ⅛ tsp. pepper

Blend the egg and onion for a few seconds in a blender. Add half the potatoes. Blend until smooth. Add the other ingredients. Blend until smooth. Drop by spoonfuls into well oiled frying pan. Fry on both sides. Drain on paper towel. Serve with apple sauce or sour cream.

Jelly Doughnuts/ Sufganiyot

Ingredients:

¾ c. orange juice or water
¼ lb. margarine
4 Tbsp. sugar
2 packages dry yeast
3 c. flour
2 eggs, beaten
Dash of salt
Vegetable oil for frying
1 cup jam
Powdered sugar

Combine orange juice, margarine, and sugar. Heat until margarine melts. Cool to lukewarm and add yeast. Stir until dissolved. Add flour, eggs, and salt. Mix and knead until smooth. (You may need to add more flour.) Place dough in a greased bowl and cover. Let rise in a warm spot for half an hour. Punch down. Shape pieces of dough into balls. Cover and let rise another half hour.

Deep fry dough balls in hot oil until golden brown. Drain on paper towels. Let cool. Fill a pastry bag with your favorite jam. Poke a hole in each donut and squeeze in a small amount of jam. Sprinkle with powdered sugar.

Reminder: Cooking with hot oil can be very dangerous. Make sure that a grown-up is helping.

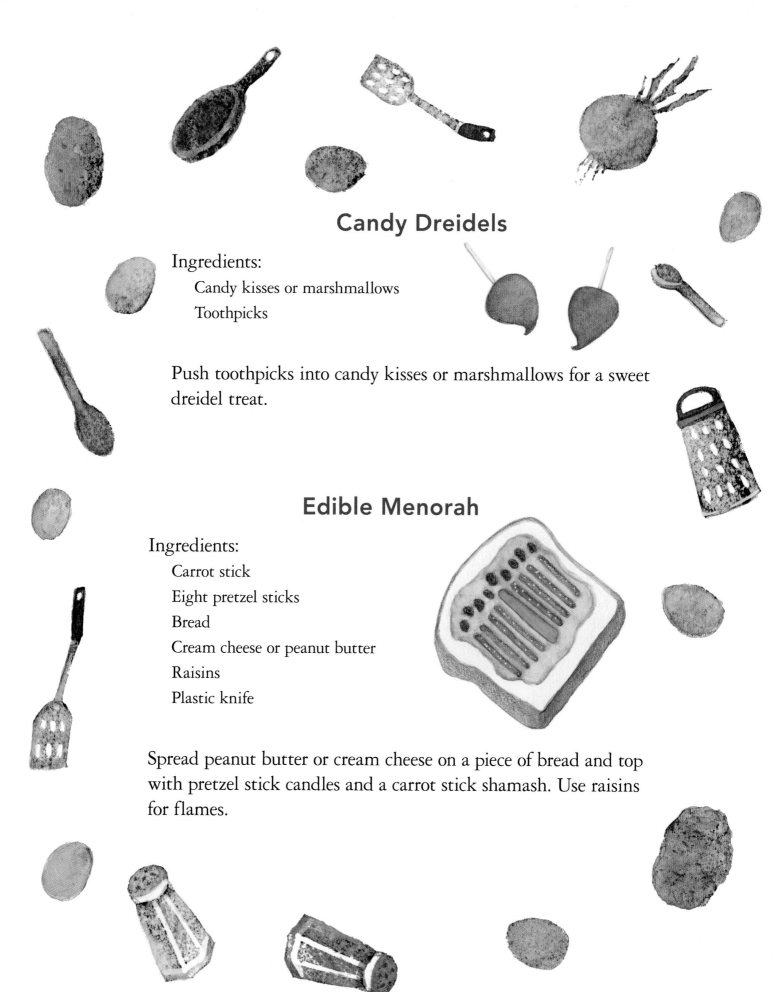

Candy Dreidels

Ingredients:
- Candy kisses or marshmallows
- Toothpicks

Push toothpicks into candy kisses or marshmallows for a sweet dreidel treat.

Edible Menorah

Ingredients:
- Carrot stick
- Eight pretzel sticks
- Bread
- Cream cheese or peanut butter
- Raisins
- Plastic knife

Spread peanut butter or cream cheese on a piece of bread and top with pretzel stick candles and a carrot stick shamash. Use raisins for flames.

HANUKKAH CRAFTS

Paper Chain Menorah

What You Need:

      Strips of colored paper

      Scissors

      Glue or stapler

      Masking tape or pins

What You Do:

1. Staple or glue one strip together to form a ring. Put another strip through the ring and fasten it to make another ring. Make a large chain of rings for the outer part of your menorah. Make smaller chains for each branch.

2. Use masking tape to attach your menorah to a window or a wall, or pin it to a curtain.

A Menorah You Can "Light"

What You Need:

    Large cardboard roll
    Paper cup with flat bottom
    Ten popsicle sticks
    Yellow tissue paper
    Paints, glue, scissors

What You Do:

1. With the scissors, make nine slits across the top of a cardboard tube. Glue the tube to the paper cup. Decorate.

2. Paint the popsicle sticks. Glue two of them together to make the tall shamash. Paste yellow tissue paper to the top of each stick for flames.

3. Place your shamash in the menorah and add one candle each night of Hanukkah.

A Coupon Gift Book

What You Need:

    Construction paper

    Scissors, stapler, markers, or crayons

What You Do:

1. Fold two pieces of construction paper in thirds and cut along folded lines. This is enough for five coupons and a cover.

2. Write or draw a promise on each coupon. Decorate the cover.

Hanging Dreidel Decoration

What You Need:

    White cardboard

    Colored paper

    Thread or thin yarn

    Scissors, glue, markers

What You Do:

1. Draw and cut out a large dreidel shape from the cardboard. Draw a smaller dreidel shape inside the big one, and cut out the inside dreidel.

2. Cut four small dreidel shapes from different colored paper. Cut four pieces of yarn or thread. Glue one end to each small dreidel and the other to the big dreidel frame.

3. Glue a long piece of yarn to the handle of the large dreidel and hang.

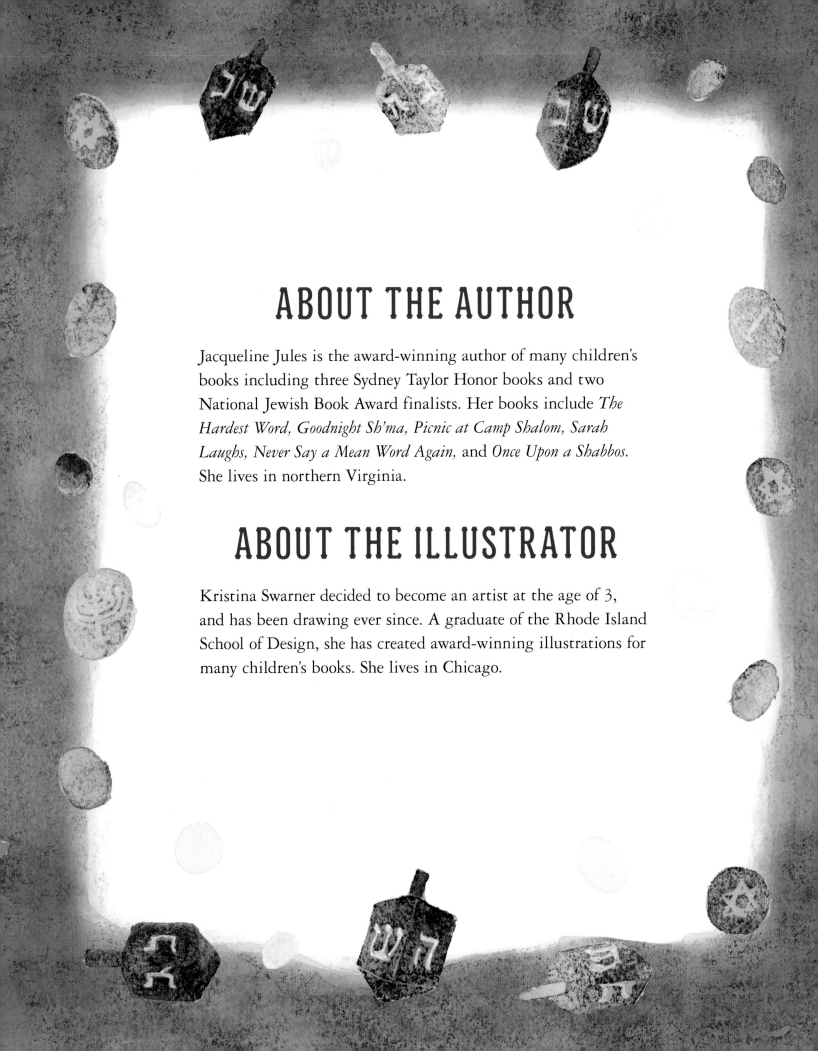

ABOUT THE AUTHOR

Jacqueline Jules is the award-winning author of many children's books including three Sydney Taylor Honor books and two National Jewish Book Award finalists. Her books include *The Hardest Word, Goodnight Sh'ma, Picnic at Camp Shalom, Sarah Laughs, Never Say a Mean Word Again,* and *Once Upon a Shabbos.* She lives in northern Virginia.

ABOUT THE ILLUSTRATOR

Kristina Swarner decided to become an artist at the age of 3, and has been drawing ever since. A graduate of the Rhode Island School of Design, she has created award-winning illustrations for many children's books. She lives in Chicago.